14 COLLECT[ED] INTERMEDIATE QUINTETS

THE CANADIAN BRASS

HAL•LEONARD®

GAVOTTE

Trumpet in B-flat I   from Suite for Unaccompanied Violoncello No. 6 in D Major, BWV 1012

Arranged by Henry Charles Smith

Johann Sebastian Bach
(1685-1750)

Copyright © 1989 by HAL LEONARD PUBLISHING CORPORATION
International Copyright Secured ALL RIGHTS RESERVED Printed in the U.S.A.

PRAYER
(Abendsegen)
from *Hänsel und Gretel*

Trumpet in B-flat I

Arranged by Henry Charles Smith

Engelbert Humperdinck
(1854-1921)

Copyright © 1989 by HAL LEONARD PUBLISHING CORPORATION
International Copyright Secured ALL RIGHTS RESERVED Printed in the U.S.A.

CANTATE DOMINO

from *Musica Divina*

Trumpet in B-flat I

Arranged by Henry Charles Smith

Giuseppe Ottavio Pitoni
(1657-1743)

Allegro ♩ = 144 (in buoyant style)

*Play the piece twice through; no ritard. nor fermata the first time.

Copyright © 1989 by HAL LEONARD PUBLISHING CORPORATION
International Copyright Secured ALL RIGHTS RESERVED Printed in the U.S.A.

THE LIBERTY BELL

Trumpet in B-flat I

Arranged by Henry Charles Smith

John Philip Sousa
(1854-1932)

Copyright © 1989 by HAL LEONARD PUBLISHING CORPORATION
International Copyright Secured ALL RIGHTS RESERVED Printed in the U.S.A.

THE DRUNKEN SAILOR

Trumpet in B-flat I

Arranged by Terry Vosbein

Traditional

Copyright © 1989 by HAL LEONARD PUBLISHING CORPORATION
International Copyright Secured ALL RIGHTS RESERVED Printed in the U.S.A.

GREENSLEEVES

Trumpet in B-flat I

Arranged by Terry Vosbein

Traditional

Copyright © 1989 by HAL LEONARD PUBLISHING CORPORATION
International Copyright Secured ALL RIGHTS RESERVED Printed in the U.S.A.

HAVA NAGILA

Trumpet in B-flat I

Arranged by Walter Barnes

Traditional

© Copyright 1988 Dr. Brass (BMI), Toronto
All Rights reserved. Printed in U.S.A.
Unauthorized copying, arranging, recording or public performance is an infringement of copyright.
Infringers are liable under the law.

HIGH BARBARY

Trumpet in B-flat I

Arranged by Terry Vosbein

Traditional

Copyright © 1989 by HAL LEONARD PUBLISHING CORPORATION
International Copyright Secured ALL RIGHTS RESERVED Printed in the U.S.A.

JUST A CLOSER WALK

Trumpet in B-flat I

Arranged by Don Gillis
Adapted by Walter Barnes

Traditional

© Copyright 1988 Dr. Brass (BMI), Toronto
All Rights reserved. Printed in U.S.A.
Unauthorized copying, arranging, recording or public performance is an infringement of copyright.
Infringers are liable under the law.

LONDONDERRY AIR

Trumpet in B-flat I

Arranged by Terry Vosbein

Traditional

Copyright © 1989 by HAL LEONARD PUBLISHING CORPORATION
International Copyright Secured ALL RIGHTS RESERVED Printed in the U.S.A.

SHENANDOAH

Trumpet in B-flat I

Arranged by Terry Vosbein

Traditional

Copyright © 1989 by HAL LEONARD PUBLISHING CORPORATION
International Copyright Secured ALL RIGHTS RESERVED Printed in the U.S.A.

SIMPLE GIFTS

Trumpet in B-flat I

Arranged by Terry Vosbein

Traditional

Copyright © 1989 by HAL LEONARD PUBLISHING CORPORATION
International Copyright Secured ALL RIGHTS RESERVED Printed in the U.S.A.

THIS AND THAT
(Questo e quella)
from *Rigoletto*

Trumpet in B-flat I

Arranged by Henry Charles Smith

Giuseppe Verdi
(1813-1901)

Copyright © 1989 by HAL LEONARD PUBLISHING CORPORATION
International Copyright Secured ALL RIGHTS RESERVED Printed in the U.S.A.

PILGRIM'S CHORUS
from *Tannhäuser und der Sängerkrieg auf Wartburg*

Trumpet in B-flat I

Arranged by Henry Charles Smith

Richard Wagner
(1813-1883)

Copyright © 1989 by HAL LEONARD PUBLISHING CORPORATION
International Copyright Secured ALL RIGHTS RESERVED Printed in the U.S.A.

CONTENTS

JOHANN SEBASTIAN BACH

ENGELBERT HUMPERDINCK

GIUSEPPE OTTAVIO PITONI

JOHN PHILIP SOUSA

TRADITIONAL

GIUSEPPE VERDI

RICHARD WAGNER

SCORE AND PARTS AVAILABLE SEPARATELY:

Conductor's Score	50486959
Trumpet 2 in B-flat	50486955
Horn in F	50486956
Trombone	50486957
Tuba	50486958

ALSO AVAILABLE IN THIS SERIES:

17 Collected Easy Quintets	50486953

8-84088-39308-3

HL50486954

HAL•LEONARD®
CORPORATION
7777 W. BLUEMOUND RD. P.O. BOX 13819 MILWAUKEE, WI 53213

www.canbrass.com
www.halleonard.com

U.S. $14.99

ISBN 978-1-4234-8421-9

51499